BUILDING
HENRY'S
BRIDGE

Building Henry's Bridge

Henry was a 10-year-old boy who loved to build things. His room was full of blocks, toy cars, and little gadgets he had made from old pieces of this and that. Henry had a big imagination, and he could spend hours dreaming up fantastic inventions and grand designs. But there was something else about Henry which made things a little tricky that Henry wasn't just known for his creativity he had ADHD.

ADHD, meant that Henry's mind was like a butterfly,

flitting from one idea to another. He could dream up grand designs, but staying focused, organized, and completing tasks was like trying to catch that elusive butterfly.

His thoughts would zip and zoom like race cars, making it tricky to finish what he started. But Henry was also smart and creative, and he always tried his best.

At the start of the school year, Henry's teacher, Mr. Thompson, announced an exciting new project. "Class, we're going to build model bridges!" he declared, his eyes twinkling with enthusiasm.

"Each of you will design and construct your own bridge, and at the end of the term, you'll present it to the class. "You can choose any type of bridge you like. This project will help us learn about structure, creativity, and perseverance."

Henry's heart skipped a beat. Bridges! He loved bridges their shapes, their strength, and the way they connected one place to another. He could already see it in his mind—a magnificent suspension bridge with tall towers and strong cables.

"Yes!" Henry whispered to himself, feeling a thrill of excitement. He couldn't wait to get started. He imagined the bridge standing proudly on display, with everyone marveling at his creation.

Yet, a shadow of doubt crept into his mind. He remembered other times when he'd started big projects. Often, his enthusiasm would carry him only so far before the distractions crept in. His room would become a jumble of half-finished projects, and he'd feel overwhelmed, unsure of how to move forward.

Shaking off the worry, Henry focused on the thrill of the new challenge. He told himself this time would be different. He would build the most amazing bridge anyone had ever seen!

The project was a chance for Henry to shine, to show his creativity and determination. He was excited to get started, but deep down, he knew it would take more than just enthusiasm to see it through. He would need to stay focused, organized, and most importantly, believe in himself every step of the way.

When Henry got home, he ran to his room and grabbed his favorite notebook. He started sketching his ideas, drawing tall towers and long cables.

While sketching the thought bubble appears above Henry's head. "Wow, these towers need to be super tall to support the cables! Maybe I can add some cool decorations on top... hmmm, what if I added a mini flag that waves in the wind?

But wait, what kind of cables should I use? String? Maybe fishing line would be stronger..."

His excitement grew with each pencil stroke. "This is going to be the best bridge ever!" he thought.

While drawing, Henry's foot starts tapping a frantic rhythm against the floor. He gets up to sharpen his pencil, but instead, gets sidetracked by a toy car on his shelf, picking it up and zooming it around the room.

But as the afternoon went on, Henry began to feel overwhelmed. His desk was covered in papers, pencils, and books. He had so many ideas, but he didn't know where to start. He wanted to research different types of bridges, but the pile of books on his desk just seemed to grow. He opened a book on suspension bridges, but after a few pages, he got distracted by the colorful illustrations of other bridges.

He put the book down and picked up another one about arch bridges. "Wait, what if I could make it a arch bridges? That would be awesome!"

But then his phone buzzed with a message from his friend Emma, and he forgot about the book. "Oh no! Emma texted! Gotta answer her right away!" He grabs his phone without finishing his current thought on bridges. But before he knew it, he was scrolling through funny videos. He loses track of time, laughing hysterically, completely forgetting about the bridge project until the phone notification sound snaps him back to reality.

"Huh? What time is it?"

When Henry finally looked up from his phone, the sun was setting, and his desk was still a mess. Papers were everywhere, and he hadn't made any real progress on his bridge. His heart sank. "How am I ever going to finish this?" he wondered aloud.

Henry's initial excitement fades as he watches the minute's tick by without making progress. His thoughts replaced by a creeping tide of self-doubt.

"Look at this mess! There's no way I can turn this into anything cool".

He slumped back in his chair, letting out a defeated sigh. "This always happens," he muttered to himself, his voice laced with frustration.

"I get all fired up at first, but then I just get lost and everything falls apart".

He picked up a crumpled drawing of a bridge with impossibly tall towers that tilted precariously at an angle. "See, I told myself I could do it, but it just looks stupid."

"Maybe I'm just not good at this kind of stuff".

A wave of negativity washed over him. Memories of past projects surfaced in his mind - a half-built robot missing an arm, a fort made of blankets that collapsed under its own weight, a model airplane that resembled a mangled bird. Each failure felt like a confirmation of his inner critic's voice.

But then, a flicker of defiance sparked in his eyes. He balled up the crumpled drawing and tossed it into his recycling bin.

"No way," he said with a newfound determination.

"Okay, maybe I got a little sidetracked, but that doesn't mean I can't get back on track".

He took a deep breath, trying to clear the fog of negativity.

"I can do this," he whispered, a sliver of hope peeking through the clouds of doubt.

It was so hard to keep his mind from wandering. After what felt like hours, he looked around and saw that he had barely made any progress. The frustration built up inside him, and he let out a big sigh.

Hearing the sigh, Henry's mom walked into his room. She could see the mess and the frown on Henry's face. She sat down next to him, gently placing a hand on his shoulder.

"Hey, buddy," she said softly. "What's going on?"

Henry looked up at her with tears in his eyes. "I don't know, Mom," he whispered, his voice cracking. I just can't seem to focus. Every time I start working on my bridge project, I get distracted or overwhelmed. It feels impossible."

His mom hugged him tightly. "I know it's tough, Henry. ADHD can make it really hard to stay focused and organized. But we can find a way to make it easier for you."

Henry sniffled and nodded. He trusted his mom and knew she always had good ideas. She reached over and picked up a blank piece of paper and a pen.

"Let's make a plan together," she said. "We'll call it the 'Roadmap to Bridge Building.' It'll help you see each step you need to take and make the project feel less overwhelming."

His mom drew a big rectangle on the paper and wrote "Henry's Roadmap to Bridge Building" at the top in big, colorful letters. Henry smiled a little at how bright and cheerful it looked.

"Okay," she continued, "let's break down your project into smaller steps. What's the first thing you need to do?"

Henry thought for a moment. "I need to finish my research. I need to know more about how bridges are built."

"Great!" his mom said, writing "Research Bridges" as the first step. "What comes next?"

"Um, I guess I need to draw my bridge design," Henry replied.

His mom added "Draw Bridge Design" to the list.

They continued like this, breaking the project into smaller tasks: "Gather Materials," "Build the Base," "Construct the Towers," and "Attach the Cables."

"Now," his mom said, "let's give each task a timeline. How long do you think you need for each step?"

They talked it over and decided on a timeline for each task. "Research Bridges" would take a few days, "Draw Bridge Design" would take one day, and so on. His mom wrote the timelines next to each task.

When they were done, Henry looked at the roadmap. It didn't seem so impossible anymore. Each step felt manageable, and seeing it all laid out made him feel more in control.

"This looks great, Mom," Henry said, feeling a spark of hope. "I think I can do this."

"I know you can, Henry," his mom replied, giving him another hug. "Remember, it's okay to take breaks and ask for help when you need it. You're not alone in this."

Henry took a deep breath and smiled. With his roadmap in hand, he felt ready to tackle his bridge project again. The sense of determination returned, and he knew he had the support he needed to succeed.

That night, as Henry got ready for bed, his mom tucked him in and shared a little poem to help him remember his roadmap:

**"When things get tough and you feel stuck,
Take a step back, don't press your luck.
Break it down and take your time,
Step by step, you'll be just fine.
With a plan and a smile so bright,
You'll build your bridge with all your might.
Remember, Henry, you're brave and strong,
With your roadmap, you can't go wrong."**

Henry drifted off to sleep, the words of the poem dancing in his mind. He dreamed of bridges and plans, feeling confident that he could handle whatever came next.

One bright Monday morning, as Henry shuffled into the classroom, Mr. Thompson noticed the determined but tired look on his face. After class, Mr. Thompson called Henry over to his desk.

"Henry, I can see you're really trying hard with your project," he said with a kind smile. "How's it going?"

Henry sighed. "I'm trying, Mr. Thompson, but it's hard to stay focused. I get distracted and then I fall behind."

Mr. Thompson nodded thoughtfully. "I understand. Have you ever tried using a schedule? It can help you know exactly when to work and when to take breaks."

That evening, Henry and his mom sat down together at the kitchen table. They spread out colored markers, paper, and a big calendar.

"Okay, Henry," his mom said, "let's make a daily schedule. We'll plan times for you to work on your project and times for breaks."

Henry's mom drew a big chart with each day of the week and lots of colorful boxes. They decided on short, focused work periods with fun breaks in between.

"In the morning, you can work on your project for 20 minutes," she explained, "then take a 10-minute break to play with Shadow or have a snack. After your break, you can work for another 20 minutes."

Henry grinned. "That sounds good! I think I can do that."

To help keep track of time, Henry's mom gave him a small kitchen timer. They set it together, and when the timer dinged, it was time for a break. Henry also made a big colorful checklist of all the tasks he needed to do for his project.

They stuck the schedule and checklist on the wall next to Henry's desk. Henry loved the bright colors and felt excited to start using them.

Each day, Henry followed his new schedule. He worked on his bridge for 20 minutes, then took breaks to play with Shadow or draw pictures. When he finished a task, he checked it off his list, feeling proud each time.

One afternoon, while working on the bridge, Henry started feeling frustrated. He was trying to cut pieces of cardboard, but they just wouldn't fit right. The timer dinged, signaling a break.

"Mom, I'm not done yet!" Henry exclaimed, annoyed.

"That's okay, Henry," his mom reassured him. "Take your break, and when you come back, you'll feel better and be able to work on it with a fresh mind."

Reluctantly, Henry took his break. He played fetch with Shadow in the backyard, running around and laughing. When he came back, he felt calmer and more focused. The cardboard pieces seemed easier to cut now, and he soon had them fitting perfectly.

As the days passed, Henry noticed something amazing. By following his schedule and using the timer, he was getting more done! The bridge was starting to take shape, and each piece fit just right. He felt a sense of pride and accomplishment with each new step.

One evening, Henry's mom peeked into his room. She saw him working diligently, the timer ticking softly in the background, and the colorful checklist almost completely filled with checkmarks.

"You're doing great, Henry," she said, giving him a

hug. "Look how much you've done!"

Henry beamed. "Thanks, Mom. I feel like I can really do this."

To help Henry remember his schedule, his mom came up with a little poem:

**"Work for a while, then take a break,
When you come back, more progress you'll make.
Check off your tasks, one by one,
Soon you'll see, your project's done!"**

Henry loved the poem and often recited it to himself while working. It made the whole process feel like a fun game.

With his new schedule and tools, Henry was building more than just a bridge—he was building confidence in himself and learning how to manage his ADHD. He was excited to see his project grow each day, and he knew he could do it.

One sunny afternoon, Henry sat at his desk with a determined look on his face. He had his roadmap in front of him and a list of tasks to complete. But where to start? Henry scratched his head and looked at the first task: "Research the strongest materials for bridge building."

"Okay, I can do this," he whispered to himself.

Henry remembered what Mr. Thompson had told him about prioritizing. "Focus on the most important parts first," his teacher had said. Henry decided that learning about the materials was the best place to begin.

He opened his book and started reading about steel, wood, and concrete. Henry read how steel was strong and could hold a lot of weight. Wood was light but not as strong, and concrete was heavy but very durable.

But then, his phone buzzed. A message from Emma, his best friend, flashed on the screen. It was a funny video of her dog, Shadow. Henry giggled and almost got sucked into watching more videos, but then he remembered his plan.

"Time to use the focus box," Henry said with a smile. He took his phone and placed it in a shoebox he had decorated with colorful stickers and called it his "focus box." He closed the lid and set a timer for 20 minutes. Until the timer beeped, no phone, no distractions.

With the focus box working its magic, Henry turned back to his book. He made notes about the strengths and weaknesses of each material. When the timer finally beeped, Henry looked at his notes and felt a rush of pride. He had completed his first task!

"Yes! I did it!" Henry cheered, punching the air with his fist.

He marked the task as done on his roadmap, drawing a big, happy checkmark next to it. Then, he set his timer for a 10-minute break. Henry danced around his room, played a quick game with his dog, and even had a snack.

When the break was over, Henry was ready for the next task: "Design the bridge supports." He had learned that the supports were the most important part of the bridge. They had to be strong and sturdy to hold everything up.

Henry sketched out different designs on a big sheet of paper. He tried a few ideas before deciding on a tall, triangular shape that looked both strong and cool. He used his toy blocks to build a small model of the supports, testing how much weight they could hold.

With each step, Henry felt more confident. He was making real progress, and it felt amazing. He could see his bridge taking shape, bit by bit, piece by piece. And all it took was a plan, some focus, and a little bit of help from his friends and family.

As the day ended, Henry looked at his roadmap and saw all the checkmarks he had made. He smiled, feeling proud of his hard work. He was one step closer to finishing his big bridge project.

One sunny afternoon, Henry was in his room, fully engrossed in constructing the middle section of his bridge. He had carefully glued popsicle sticks together to form the sturdy beams and was just adding the final touches when he heard Shadow, his playful dog, bark loudly.

Startled, Henry turned around, and in that brief moment, his hand accidentally knocked over a bottle of glue. The glue spilled onto the half-finished bridge, causing it to collapse.

Henry's heart sank. He watched in dismay as the structure he had worked so hard on fell apart. Tears welled up in his eyes. "Why does this always happen to me?" he thought. "I try so hard, but nothing ever goes right."

Henry's mom, hearing the commotion, came into his

room. She saw the broken bridge and Henry's tear-streaked face.

Kneeling down, she wrapped her arms around him. "It's okay, Henry. We all make mistakes and face setbacks. The important thing is how we handle them."

Henry sniffled, "But I was so close! Now it's ruined!"

His mom smiled gently, "It's not ruined. It's just a small setback. Let's take a deep breath together."

She placed her hands on her belly and took a slow, deep breath, showing Henry how to do the same. Henry mimicked her, feeling the air fill his lungs and then slowly exhaling. They repeated this a few times until Henry felt a little calmer.

His mom then walked over to the "Roadmap to Bridge Building" chart they had made together. She pointed to the steps they had already completed. "Look, Henry. You've done so much already. You've researched, you've gathered materials, and you've built the foundation. This is just a small bump in the road."

Henry looked at the chart, and a tiny spark of hope flickered inside him. "I guess you're right. But what should I do now?"

His mom said, "First, let's clean up this mess. Then we can see how to fix the bridge. Remember, we have a plan, and setbacks are just part of the journey. Each time you overcome a challenge, you get stronger and smarter."

With his mom's help, Henry cleaned up the spilled glue and assessed the damage. Some parts of the bridge were still intact, but others needed to be rebuilt. They carefully removed the damaged sections and laid out the pieces that could be reused.

As they worked, his mom said, "Sometimes, when things don't go as planned, we find better ways to do them. Maybe this is an opportunity to make your bridge even stronger."

Henry nodded, feeling a bit more determined. He thought about how he could reinforce the beams and make the structure more stable. With fresh ideas and renewed energy, he started rebuilding the bridge, this time paying extra attention to each connection.

Henry stood in his room, looking at the pieces of his bridge scattered all around him. He took a deep breath and reminded himself of his roadmap. The first task for today was to gather all the materials he needed. He grabbed his checklist and started ticking off items one by one.

"Wooden sticks, check. Glue, check. Cardboard, check," Henry muttered to himself. He even had some old toy parts that he thought might come in handy. With everything laid out in front of him, Henry felt ready to begin.

Henry knew the base of the bridge was the most important part. It had to be strong enough to hold everything together. He carefully cut the cardboard into two long strips.

"Let's make them strong, not too long," he rhymed, smiling at his little song.

He glued the wooden sticks to the cardboard, making sure they were evenly spaced. He pressed them down firmly and waited for the glue to dry. While waiting, Henry hummed a tune to keep himself from getting distracted.

Next, Henry turned his attention to the towers. He used the recycled materials he had collected: some old plastic tubes from a toy construction set. He measured and cut the tubes to the right height, making sure they were exactly the same length.

"Measure twice, cut once, that's how it's done!" he chanted, enjoying the rhythm of his work.

Henry glued the towers onto the base, ensuring they were straight and secure. He used some extra cardboard pieces to reinforce the bottom, making them even sturdier.

As the sun began to set, Henry stepped back to look at his bridge. It wasn't finished, but it was back on track. He felt a sense of accomplishment for having overcome the setback.

For the suspension cables, Henry used some thick

string he had found in his dad's toolbox. He tied one end of the string to the top of the tower and the other end to the base. He repeated this for each tower, making sure the strings were tight.

"Pull it tight, not too light, let's get it right!" he rhymed again, finding comfort in the repetition.

The strings crisscrossed each other, forming a web of support. Henry stood back to admire his work. The bridge was starting to look real.

The last major part was the roadway. Henry cut a piece of cardboard to fit between the towers. He carefully slid it into place and glued it down, making sure it was level and secure.

Now came the fun part—decorating the bridge! Henry found some old paint and decided to give his bridge a bit of color. He painted the towers bright red and the roadway a cool gray. He added tiny flags made from paper and toothpicks to the tops of the towers, giving his bridge a festive look.

"Red and gray, paint away, flags to sway," he sang happily.

Henry checked his roadmap to make sure he hadn't missed anything. Everything was in place, but he knew there was one final step—testing the bridge. He gently pressed down on the roadway, feeling it give just a little but staying strong.

"Strong and steady, bridge is ready!" he declared, feeling a rush of pride.

As Henry looked at his nearly completed bridge, he felt a mix of emotions—excitement, pride, and a little bit of nervousness about the final presentation. But most of all, he felt a sense of accomplishment. His hard work, patience, and the strategies he had learned had paid off. The bridge was a symbol of his creativity and determination.

Henry couldn't wait to show it to his family and friends. He knew that no matter what happened next, he had already achieved something amazing. His bridge was a testament to his ability to focus, stay organized, and see a project through to the end.

"Henry's bridge, standing tall, built with care, won't let me fall," he whispered, smiling to himself.

Throughout the process, his mom continued to encourage him. "You're doing great, Henry. Look how strong this section is now. You're learning and improving every step of the way."

"Thanks, Mom," he said, hugging her tightly. "I

couldn't have done it without you."

His mom smiled, "You did it yourself, Henry. I just helped you see how strong and capable you are. Remember, the roadmap is there to guide you, but your determination is what makes it happen."

The day of the big presentation finally arrived. Henry woke up with a fluttering feeling in his stomach, a mix of excitement and nervousness. He looked at his model bridge, standing tall and proud on his desk, and took a deep breath. "I can do this," he whispered to himself.

Henry's mom helped him get ready, reminding him to breathe deeply and stay calm. "Remember, Henry, you've worked so hard on this. Just share your story and show them your amazing bridge," she said, giving him a reassuring hug.

At school, the classroom buzzed with excitement. All the students had brought their projects, and Mr. Thompson had set up a special area for presentations. Henry carefully carried his bridge into the room, placing it on the designated table.

As Henry waited for his turn, he felt the butterflies in his stomach flutter even more. He glanced around and saw Emma, his best friend, giving him a thumbs-up from across the room. That made him smile a little.

Finally, Mr. Thompson called Henry's name. "Next up, we have Henry with his suspension bridge project!" he announced. Henry took another deep breath, picked up his project, and walked to the front of the class.

Henry stood in front of his classmates, holding his model bridge. He felt his hands tremble a bit, but he remembered his mom's advice. "Hi, everyone," he began, "this is my suspension bridge. I want to tell you how I built it and what I learned."

As Henry started talking, his nervousness began to fade. He explained how he had chosen a suspension bridge because he loved how strong and flexible they were. He described the different parts of his bridge, like the towers, cables, and deck, using simple words so everyone could understand.

Henry held up the roadmap he had used to plan his project. "This roadmap helped me a lot," he said. "I broke my project into small steps, like researching bridges, gathering materials, and building each part one at a time. It kept me on track and made everything less scary."

He also shared some of the challenges he faced. "Sometimes, I got distracted or things didn't go as planned. My bridge even collapsed once!" he said, with a small laugh. "But I didn't give up. I used my roadmap to remember what I needed to do next, and I took breaks to clear my mind."

To make his presentation more fun, Henry used some poem he had come up with:

**"When the cables were a mess, I didn't stress,
I took a break, for goodness' sake!
With my roadmap in my hand, I knew where to land."**

His classmates giggled and clapped at the rhymes, and Henry felt his confidence grow.

He then carefully showed everyone his bridge, pointing out how he used recycled materials to build it. "These towers are made from old toy blocks, and the cables are string I found at home," he explained. "It's not just a bridge, it's a creative bridge!"

When he finished, the room was filled with applause. Mr. Thompson smiled warmly. "Fantastic job, Henry! You showed us not just a great bridge, but also how you used planning and perseverance to succeed."

As the presentations ended, Mr. Thompson stood up to announce the awards. "The award for 'Best Overall Project' goes to... Henry, for his outstanding suspension bridge!"

Henry's heart soared with pride as he walked up to receive his award. He looked at his classmates and felt an overwhelming sense of accomplishment. He had done it! All the hard work, the planning, and the overcoming of obstacles had paid off.

That evening, as Henry and his family celebrated at home, he looked at his model bridge one more time. It wasn't just a school project; it was a symbol of his hard work, creativity, and determination. Henry knew that if he could build a bridge, he could do anything he set his mind to.

And with that, Henry felt ready to take on whatever challenge came next, always remembering to use his roadmap and stay positive.

The afternoon sun cast a warm glow in Henry's living room as he walked in, clutching his "Best Overall Project" award. His parents greeted him with wide smiles and hugs, their pride evident in their sparkling eyes.

"Henry, you did it!" his mom exclaimed, lifting him into a tight embrace. "We're so proud of you."

Henry's heart swelled with joy. He felt like he was floating on air, his feet barely touching the ground. Shadow, his playful dog, wagged his tail furiously and barked happily, sensing the excitement in the room.

"You're the best, Shadow!" Henry giggled, kneeling down to hug his furry friend.

That evening, Henry's house buzzed with celebration. His best friend Emma arrived with a handmade card that said, "Congrats, Bridge Builder Henry!" in colorful letters. She handed it to him with a beaming smile.

"Thanks, Emma! This means a lot," Henry said, feeling a warm glow in his chest.

Emma grinned. "You worked so hard, Henry. You deserve it!"

The room was filled with laughter and cheer as Henry's parents brought out a cake shaped like a bridge. "To Henry, our brilliant builder!" his dad announced, and everyone clapped and cheered.

They all sang a playful rhyme together:
"Henry built a bridge, sturdy and true,
With focus and hard work, he saw it through.
He faced every challenge, big and small,
Now he stands proud, the tallest of all!"

Henry couldn't stop smiling. The cake was delicious, and the room was filled with joy and pride. Shadow danced around their feet, enjoying the happy atmosphere.

Later, as the celebration wound down and guests began to leave, Henry sat quietly by the model bridge he had built. He ran his fingers along its sturdy frame, remembering the journey it had taken to build it.

His mom joined him, sitting down on the floor. "Thinking about your bridge?" she asked gently.

Henry nodded. "Yeah, Mom. It wasn't easy, but I did it."

She smiled. "You did, Henry. And you learned so much along the way."

Henry thought about the roadmap they had created,

the daily schedules, and the focus box. "I learned to make a plan and stick to it," he said slowly. "And when things got tough, I didn't give up."

His mom nodded. "That's right. You stayed positive and kept going, even when it was hard."

Henry looked at her, a question forming in his mind. "Do you think I can use these strategies for other things too?"

His mom's eyes sparkled with pride. "Absolutely, Henry. Your bridge is more than just a school project. It's a symbol of how you can overcome challenges with the right tools and mindset. You can use these strategies for anything you set your mind to."

Henry smiled, feeling a warm glow inside. He looked at the bridge again, seeing it not just as a model but as a symbol of his journey. It reminded him that he could face any challenge, as long as he stayed focused, organized, and positive.

And so, with a heart full of hope and a mind ready for the next adventure, Henry stepped into the new day, knowing that his journey had just begun.

Reflection Questions!

What did Henry do when he felt overwhelmed by the big project?

When Henry felt overwhelmed by his big bridge project, he struggled with staying focused and organizing his work. His room was messy, he got distracted easily, and he felt frustrated because he couldn't see how to complete the project. This made him feel like giving up.

To solve this problem, Henry's mom and his teacher helped him by breaking down the project into smaller, manageable steps and creating a clear plan with timelines. This "Roadmap to Bridge Building" made the task seem less overwhelming and helped him stay on track.

How did taking breaks help Henry stay focused?

Taking breaks helped Henry rest his mind and come back to his project with fresh energy. It made it easier for him to stay focused without feeling too tired or distracted.

Can you remember a time when you had a big project or task? How did you feel?

Think about a time when you had a big job to do, like a school project or cleaning your room. At first, it might have felt overwhelming or hard to start. You might have felt stressed or unsure if you could finish it. This is similar to how Henry felt with his bridge project.

Why is it important to stay positive, even when things don't go as planned?

Staying positive helps you keep going, even when things get tough. When you focus on what's going well and believe that you can solve problems, you're more likely to find solutions and keep working towards your goal. If Henry had given up when his bridge collapsed, he wouldn't have been able to finish it. By staying positive and using his roadmap, he could fix the problems and complete his project.

Activity: Create Your Own Roadmap!

Step 1: PICK A GOAL

Think about something big you want to accomplish. Is it cleaning your room? Finishing a book? Or maybe starting your own cool project, like building something or learning a new skill? Write down your goal at the end of your roadmap, just like Henry's bridge was at the end of his.

Step 2: BREAK IT DOWN

Now, think about all the little steps you need to take to reach your goal. What's the first thing you need to do? What comes next? Write down each step along your roadmap. For example, if your goal is to clean your room, your steps might be:

- Pick up toys.
- Put clothes in the laundry.
- Organize books and papers.
- Vacuum the floor.

Step 3: SET A TIMER

Decide how long you'll spend on each step. It could be 10 minutes or 20 minutes — whatever feels right to you. Remember, it's okay to take breaks! Just like Henry, set a timer so you stay on track. Maybe you work for 20 minutes and then take a 5-minute break to stretch or grab a snack.

Step 4: FOCUS BOX

Find a box, bin, or a special place where you can put anything that might distract you while you're working. It could be your favorite toys, games, or even your tablet. This is your "Focus Box." When you're done with your task, you can take them out again!

Step 5: CELEBRATE

When you've finished all your steps, give yourself a high-five, just like Henry did! You worked hard, and now it's time to celebrate. You can treat yourself to something fun, like playing with a favorite toy, reading a book, or sharing your accomplishment with your family.

Activity: Jamie's Solar System Project

Jamie has a big science fair project to complete. He needs to build a model of the solar system, but he feels overwhelmed. Jamie has trouble staying focused, and he keeps getting distracted by his phone and other activities. He doesn't know where to start or how to manage his time effectively. As a result, he feels frustrated and anxious about finishing the project on time.

INTERACTIVE CHALLENGE:

HOW WOULD YOU HELP JAMIE WITH HIS SCIENCE FAIR PROJECT?

- What small steps can Jamie take to build his model of the solar system?
- How can Jamie use a timer to stay focused on each part of the project?
- What are some ways Jamie can keep his phone and other distractions away while he works?
- How can Jamie reward himself for completing each step of his project?

Step 1: BREAK IT DOWN!

Jamie could start by making a list of all the parts of the solar system model, like the sun, planets, and orbits. He could then plan to work on each part one at a time.

Step 2: SET A TIMER!

Jamie can set a timer for 20 minutes to work on one part of the model and then take a 5-minute break before starting the next part.

Step 3: MANAGE DISTRACTIONS!

Jamie can put his phone in a drawer or another room while he works, so he's not tempted to check it.

Step 4: CELEBRATE PROGRESS!

Jamie can treat himself to a favorite snack or activity after finishing each part of the project to keep himself motivated.

By following these steps, Jamie can manage his project better and reduce feelings of being overwhelmed, just like Henry did with his bridge project.